Top Restaurants Secret Recipes

Shahaan Merchant

Published by Sajjad Saleem, 2024.

TOP RESTAURANTS SECRET RECIPES

First edition. February 5, 2024.

ISBN: 979-8223743675

Written by Shahaan Merchant.

Table of Contents

Top Restaurants
Secret
Recipes

Shahaan Merchant

Top Restaurants Secret Recipes

Author
Shahaan Merchant

KFC - Original Recipe Fried Chicken

Here's an easy-to-follow recipe for KFC-style Fried Chicken, using halal ingredients and simple kitchen tools:

Ingredients:

- 8 pieces of chicken (thighs, drumsticks, or preferred cuts)
    - 2 cups all-purpose flour
    - 1 tbsp paprika
    - 1 tbsp garlic powder
    - 1 tbsp onion powder
    - 1 tbsp dried oregano
    - 1 tbsp chili powder (adjust to taste)
    - 1 tbsp black pepper
    - 1 tbsp salt
    - 2 cups buttermilk
    - Vegetable oil for frying

Tools Required:

- Mixing bowls
    - Deep frying pan or pot
    - Tongs
    - Wire rack
    - Paper towels

Method:

Prepare the Chicken:

- Rinse the chicken pieces and pat them dry with paper towels.

Mix the Seasonings:

- Combine flour, paprika, garlic powder, onion powder, oregano, chili powder, black pepper, and salt in a bowl. Mix well.

Soak the Chicken:

- Place chicken in a bowl and pour buttermilk over it, ensuring all pieces are coated. Let it soak for at least 20 minutes.

Coat the Chicken:

- Heat vegetable oil in a frying pan over medium-high heat (around 350°F or 175°C).

- Take each piece of chicken from the buttermilk, let excess drip off, and coat generously in the seasoned flour mixture.

Fry the Chicken:

- Carefully place coated chicken pieces in the hot oil, avoiding overcrowding. Fry for 15-20 minutes, turning occasionally until golden brown and internal temperature reaches 165°F (74°C).

Drain and Rest:

- Use tongs to remove cooked chicken from oil and place it on a wire rack lined with paper towels to drain excess oil.

Additional Tips:

- Seasoning Adjustment: Feel free to adjust the spices based on your taste preferences.
- Oil Temperature Check: Keep an eye on the oil temperature to ensure proper frying.
- Resting Time: Let the fried chicken rest for a few minutes before serving to retain its juiciness and crispiness.

This recipe aims to replicate the classic KFC-style Fried Chicken using halal ingredients, simple cooking tools, and easy-to-follow steps for a delicious homemade meal.

KFC-Style Zinger Burger Recipe

Ingredients:

- 4 boneless chicken filets
  - 4 burger buns
  - 1 cup all-purpose flour
  - 1 teaspoon paprika
  - 1 teaspoon garlic powder
  - 1 teaspoon onion powder
  - 1 teaspoon cayenne pepper
  - 1 teaspoon salt
  - 1 egg
  - 1 cup buttermilk
  - Vegetable oil for frying
  - Lettuce leaves
  - Sliced tomatoes
  - Sliced cheese (optional)

Tools Required:

- Frying pan
  - Mixing bowls
  - Tongs
  - Wire rack
  - Paper towels

Method:

Preparing the Chicken:

Flour Mixture:

- In a mixing bowl, combine flour, paprika, garlic powder, onion powder, cayenne pepper, and salt. Mix well.

Whisk the Egg and Buttermilk:

● In another bowl, whisk the egg and buttermilk together until thoroughly combined.

Coating the Chicken:

● Dip each chicken fillet into the flour mixture, then into the egg and buttermilk mixture, and again into the flour mixture to coat evenly.

Frying the Chicken:

● Heat vegetable oil in a frying pan over medium-high heat.

● Carefully place the coated chicken fillets into the hot oil and fry for about 5-6 minutes per side, or until golden brown and cooked through.

Drain and Rest:

● Once cooked, remove the chicken fillets from the oil and place them on a wire rack lined with paper towels to drain excess oil. Let them rest for a few minutes.

Assembling the Burger:

Prepare the Buns:

● Toast the burger buns lightly in a separate pan or toaster.

Layering the Ingredients:

● On the bottom half of each bun, place a lettuce leaf, followed by a slice of tomato.

● Optionally, add a slice of cheese on top of the tomato.

• Put the fried chicken fillet on top of the cheese or tomato.

Top and Serve:

• Place the top half of the bun over the chicken to complete the burger.

Additional Tips:

• For a spicier kick, increase the amount of cayenne pepper in the flour mixture.

• Experiment with different types of cheese or additional toppings to suit your taste preferences.

• You can spread a favorite sauce, such as mayonnaise or spicy sauce, on the buns for added flavor.

This homemade Zinger Burger recipe aims to replicate the flavors of the popular KFC version using halal ingredients and simple cooking tools, allowing you to enjoy this crispy and flavorful burger at home!

KFC-Style Hot Wings Recipe

Ingredients:

- 12 chicken wings
  - 1 cup all-purpose flour
  - 1 teaspoon paprika
  - 1 teaspoon garlic powder
  - 1 teaspoon onion powder
  - 1 teaspoon cayenne pepper
  - 1 teaspoon salt
  - Vegetable oil for frying
  - 1/2 cup hot sauce (like Frank's RedHot)
  - 1/4 cup unsalted butter
  - 1 tablespoon honey (optional)

Tools Required:

- Frying pan
  - Mixing bowls
  - Tongs
  - Wire rack
  - Paper towels

Method:

Preparing the Chicken Wings:

Flour Coating:

- In a mixing bowl, combine flour, paprika, garlic powder, onion powder, cayenne pepper, and salt. Mix the ingredients thoroughly.

Coating the Wings:

- Coat each chicken wing in the flour mixture, ensuring they're evenly covered.

Frying the Wings:

- Heat vegetable oil in a frying pan over medium-high heat.

- Carefully place the coated chicken wings into the hot oil and fry for about 10-12 minutes, turning occasionally until they're golden brown and fully cooked.

Drain and Rest:

- Once cooked, use tongs to remove the wings from the oil and place them on a wire rack lined with paper towels to drain excess oil. Let them rest for a few minutes.

Making the Hot Sauce:

Sauce Preparation:

- In a saucepan, combine hot sauce and unsalted butter. Optionally, add honey for a touch of sweetness.

Simmer and Stir:

- Heat the saucepan over low heat, stirring constantly until the butter melts and the ingredients combine into a smooth sauce.

Tossing the Wings in Sauce:

Coat with Hot Sauce:

- Transfer the fried wings to a large mixing bowl.

- Pour the prepared hot sauce over the wings and toss them gently until each wing is coated with the sauce.

Serve:

- Place the hot wings on a serving plate and serve them with your choice of dipping sauce or celery sticks.

Additional Tips:

- Adjust the amount of cayenne pepper or hot sauce based on your preferred level of spiciness.
- For a milder version, reduce the cayenne pepper or mix in a bit of barbecue sauce to the hot sauce.
- Serve with ranch or blue cheese dressing for dipping to balance the heat.

This homemade Hot Wings recipe aims to recreate the flavors of KFC-style wings using halal ingredients and simple kitchen tools, providing a spicy and delicious appetizer or meal option!

KFC-Style Coleslaw Recipe

Ingredients:

- 4 cups shredded cabbage
  - 1/2 cup shredded carrots
  - 1/4 cup finely chopped onion
  - 1/4 cup mayonnaise
  - 2 tablespoons granulated sugar
  - 1 tablespoon white vinegar
  - 1/4 teaspoon salt
  - 1/4 teaspoon black pepper

Tools Required:

- Mixing bowl
  - Whisk or spoon

Method:

Preparing the Coleslaw:

Mixing the Vegetables:

- In a mixing bowl, combine shredded cabbage, shredded carrots, and finely chopped onion. Toss them together gently.

Making the Dressing:

- In a separate bowl, whisk together mayonnaise, granulated sugar, white vinegar, salt, and black pepper until well combined.

Coating the Vegetables:

- Pour the prepared dressing over the cabbage mixture.

● Use a spoon or a spatula to mix until the vegetables are evenly coated with the dressing.

Chilling (Optional):

● For enhanced flavor, refrigerate the coleslaw for at least an hour before serving. This allows the flavors to meld together.

Serving:

Final Touches:

● Give the coleslaw a gentle stir before serving to ensure the dressing is evenly distributed.

Serve Cold:

● Serve the KFC-style coleslaw chilled as a refreshing side dish.

Additional Tips:

● You can adjust the sweetness or tanginess by altering the amount of sugar or vinegar according to your taste preferences.

● For added crunch, consider adding a handful of chopped nuts or seeds, like almonds or sunflower seeds.

● This coleslaw pairs well with fried chicken or sandwiches, making it a versatile side dish for various meals.

Enjoy this homemade KFC-inspired coleslaw made with halal ingredients, providing a fresh and delicious addition to your meals!

KFC-Style Potato Wedges Recipe

Ingredients:

- 4 large potatoes
  - 1/4 cup vegetable oil
  - 1 teaspoon paprika
  - 1 teaspoon garlic powder
  - 1 teaspoon onion powder
  - 1 teaspoon salt
  - 1/2 teaspoon black pepper

Tools Required:

- Baking sheet
  - Mixing bowl
  - Knife
  - Cutting board
  - Spatula or tongs

Method:

Preparing the Potatoes:

Preheat the Oven:

- Preheat your oven to 400°F (200°C) to ensure it's hot when you're ready to bake.

Washing and Cutting:

- Wash the potatoes thoroughly and pat them dry. Cut each potato into wedges by slicing it into halves, then quarters, and then cutting each quarter into wedges.

Seasoning Mixture:

- In a mixing bowl, combine vegetable oil, paprika, garlic powder, onion powder, salt, and black pepper. Mix well.

Coating the Potatoes:

- Place the potato wedges in the bowl with the seasoning mixture. Toss the wedges gently until they are evenly coated.

Baking the Potato Wedges:

Preparing the Baking Sheet:

- Line a baking sheet with parchment paper or lightly grease it to prevent sticking.

Arranging the Wedges:

- Spread the seasoned potato wedges in a single layer on the prepared baking sheet.

Baking Process:

- Place the baking sheet in the preheated oven and bake for approximately 30-35 minutes, or until the wedges are golden brown and crispy, flipping them halfway through the baking time for even cooking.

Serve Hot:

- Remove the potato wedges from the oven and let them cool for a few minutes before serving.

Additional Tips:

- Feel free to adjust the seasoning according to your taste preferences by adding more or less of the spices listed.
- For a spicier kick, consider adding a pinch of cayenne pepper or chili powder to the seasoning mixture.

● These potato wedges are great as a side dish or as a snack served with your favorite dipping sauce.

Enjoy these homemade KFC-style potato wedges made with halal ingredients, providing a crispy and flavorful addition to your meals!

KFC-Style Twister Recipe

Ingredients:

- 2 boneless chicken breasts
  - 4 large tortilla wraps
  - 1 cup iceberg lettuce, shredded
  - 1 tomato, sliced
  - 1/2 cup mayonnaise
  - 2 tablespoons hot sauce (adjust to taste)
  - 1 teaspoon garlic powder
  - 1 teaspoon onion powder
  - Salt and black pepper to taste
  - Vegetable oil for cooking

Tools Required:

- Skillet or frying pan
  - Mixing bowl
  - Tongs or spatula

Method:

Preparing the Chicken:

Chicken Preparation:

- Cut the chicken breasts into thin strips or bite-sized pieces.

Seasoning the Chicken:

- In a mixing bowl, season the chicken strips with garlic powder, onion powder, salt, and black pepper. Toss well to coat.

Cooking the Chicken:

- Heat a little vegetable oil in a skillet or frying pan over medium-high heat.

- Add the seasoned chicken strips to the hot pan and cook for about 5-7 minutes, or until they are fully cooked and golden brown. Set aside.

Making the Spicy Mayo Sauce:

Mixing the Sauce:

- In a small bowl, combine mayonnaise and hot sauce. Adjust the amount of hot sauce based on your preferred level of spiciness.

Assembling the Twisters:

Wraps Preparation:

- Lay out the tortilla wraps on a clean surface.

Layering the Ingredients:

- Spread a generous amount of the spicy mayo sauce onto each tortilla wrap.

- Place a handful of shredded lettuce on top of the sauce on each wrap.

- Add sliced tomatoes on top of the lettuce.

Adding the Chicken:

- Place the cooked chicken strips on top of the vegetables in each wrap.

Rolling the Wraps:

• Fold the sides of the tortilla wraps inwards and then roll them up tightly, securing the filling inside.

Serving:

• Serve the KFC-style Twisters immediately, or wrap them in parchment paper or foil for on-the-go enjoyment.

Additional Tips:

• Customize the fillings by adding shredded cheese, sliced onions, or your favorite veggies for added flavor and texture.

• Warm the tortilla wraps in the microwave for a few seconds before assembling to make them more pliable and easier to roll.

• Experiment with different sauces or dressings for unique flavor variations.

Enjoy these homemade KFC-style Twisters made with halal ingredients, offering a delicious handheld meal option!

KFC-Style Popcorn Chicken Recipe

Ingredients:

- 1 pound boneless chicken breasts or thighs
  - 1 cup all-purpose flour
  - 1 teaspoon paprika
  - 1 teaspoon garlic powder
  - 1 teaspoon onion powder
  - 1 teaspoon salt
  - 1/2 teaspoon black pepper
  - 1 egg
  - 1/2 cup milk
  - Vegetable oil for frying

Tools Required:

- Mixing bowls
  - Cutting board
  - Knife
  - Frying pan or deep fryer
  - Paper towels
  - Slotted spoon or tongs

Method:

Preparing the Chicken:

Chicken Cutting:

- Cut the chicken breasts or thighs into bite-sized pieces or small chunks.

Seasoned Coating:

- In a mixing bowl, combine flour, paprika, garlic powder, onion powder, salt, and black pepper. Mix the ingredients well.

Coating the Chicken:

- In another bowl, whisk together the egg and milk.

- Dip each piece of chicken into the egg mixture, allowing excess to drip off, then coat thoroughly in the seasoned flour mixture.

Frying the Popcorn Chicken:

Heating the Oil:

- Heat vegetable oil in a frying pan or deep fryer to around 350°F (175°C).

Frying Process:

- Carefully place the coated chicken pieces into the hot oil, making sure not to overcrowd the pan. Fry in batches if needed.

- Fry the chicken for about 3-4 minutes, or until golden brown and crispy, turning occasionally for even cooking.

Draining Excess Oil:

- Use a slotted spoon or tongs to transfer the fried chicken pieces to a plate lined with paper towels to absorb excess oil.

Serving:

Ready to Enjoy:

- Serve the KFC-style popcorn chicken hot with your favorite dipping sauce.

Additional Tips:

● For extra flavor, you can add additional spices or herbs to the flour mixture, such as cayenne pepper for heat or dried herbs like thyme or oregano for added aroma.

● Serve with dipping sauces like ranch, barbecue sauce, or honey mustard for a delicious treat.

Enjoy this homemade version of KFC-style popcorn chicken made with halal ingredients, perfect for a snack or as part of a meal!

KFC-Style French Fries Recipe

Ingredients:

- 4 large potatoes
  - Vegetable oil for frying
  - Salt to taste

Tools Required:

- Knife
  - Cutting board
  - Bowl
  - Frying pan or deep fryer
  - Paper towels

Method:

Preparing the Potatoes:

Washing and Peeling:

- Wash the potatoes thoroughly and peel off the skin.

Cutting into Fries:

- Cut the potatoes into thin sticks or strips, ensuring they are of uniform size for even cooking.

Soaking (Optional):

- Soak the cut potatoes in cold water for about 30 minutes to remove excess starch. Then, pat them dry with paper towels.

Frying the French Fries:

Heating the Oil:

- Heat vegetable oil in a frying pan or deep fryer to around 320°F (160°C).

First Fry:

- Carefully add the potato sticks into the oil in batches. Fry for about 4-5 minutes, until they are soft but not browned.

Draining and Cooling:

- Use a slotted spoon or basket to remove the partially cooked fries and place them on paper towels to drain excess oil. Let them cool for about 10 minutes.

Second Fry:

- Increase the oil temperature to 375°F (190°C).

- Return the partially cooked fries to the hot oil in batches. Fry for another 2-3 minutes until they turn golden brown and crispy.

Draining and Seasoning:

- Once cooked, transfer the fries to a paper towel-lined plate to drain any excess oil. Sprinkle salt over the fries while they're still hot.

Additional Tips:

- Ensure the oil is hot enough before frying to prevent the fries from becoming greasy.
- For a crisper texture, you can freeze the partially cooked fries for about 30 minutes before the second fry.
- Experiment with seasoning blends like garlic powder, paprika, or Cajun seasoning for a unique flavor twist.

Enjoy these homemade KFC-style French fries made with halal ingredients, providing a crispy and tasty side dish for your meals!

McDonald's-Style Big Mac Recipe

Ingredients:

- 2 beef burger patties
  - 3 sesame seed burger buns
  - 1/4 cup shredded lettuce
  - 2 slices American cheese
  - 2 tablespoons diced onions
  - 2 tablespoons pickles, sliced
  - 1/4 cup Big Mac Sauce (mayonnaise, ketchup, sweet pickle relish, vinegar, and spices)

Tools Required:

- Skillet or grill
  - Small mixing bowl
  - Spatula
  - Cutting board
  - Knife

Method:

Cooking the Patties:

Heating the Skillet or Grill:

- Heat a skillet or grill over medium-high heat.

Cooking the Patties:

- Place the beef patties onto the heated skillet or grill.

- Cook for approximately 3-4 minutes on each side or until they reach your preferred level of doneness.

Preparing the Burger Components:

Toasting the Buns:

- Place the burger buns on the skillet or grill, toasting them lightly until they turn golden brown.

Layering the Burger:

- On the bottom half of the bun, spread a portion of the Big Mac Sauce.
- Layer shredded lettuce on top of the sauce.
- Place a beef patty on the lettuce.
- Add a slice of American cheese on top of the patty.
- Sprinkle diced onions over the cheese.
- Add the middle bun layer.

Adding More Layers:

- Spread another portion of Big Mac Sauce on the middle bun.
- Add shredded lettuce and pickle slices.

Completing the Burger:

- Place the second beef patty on top of the pickles.
- Add the remaining top bun.

Serving:

Cutting and Serving:

- Cut the burger into quarters using a sharp knife.
- Serve the McDonald's-style Big Mac immediately.

Additional Tips:

- Customize the burger by adding or omitting ingredients to suit your taste preferences.

• The Big Mac Sauce can be made by mixing mayonnaise, ketchup, sweet pickle relish, vinegar, and a blend of spices. Adjust the ingredients to achieve the desired flavor.

Enjoy this homemade version of the McDonald's Big Mac made with halal ingredients, offering a delicious and satisfying meal!

McDonald's-Style Mac Burger Sauce Recipe

Ingredients:

- 1/2 cup mayonnaise
  - 2 tablespoons ketchup
  - 1 tablespoon sweet pickle relish
  - 1 teaspoon white vinegar
  - 1/2 teaspoon garlic powder
  - 1/2 teaspoon onion powder
  - Pinch of salt

Tools Required:

- Mixing bowl
  - Spoon

Method:

Making the Sauce:

Mixing Ingredients:

- In a mixing bowl, combine mayonnaise, ketchup, sweet pickle relish, white vinegar, garlic powder, onion powder, and a pinch of salt.

Stirring Well:

- Mix all the ingredients together thoroughly until well combined.

Adjusting Consistency (Optional):

- If the sauce is too thick, you can add a small amount of water or milk and stir until you achieve the desired consistency.

Storing the Sauce:

Transfer and Refrigerate:

- Once mixed, transfer the sauce to an airtight container or jar.

Chilling:

- Refrigerate the sauce for at least 30 minutes before serving to allow the flavors to meld together.

Additional Tips:

- Adjust the ingredients according to your taste preferences. You can add a bit more ketchup for sweetness or pickle relish for tanginess.
- This sauce pairs perfectly with burgers, sandwiches, or even as a dipping sauce for fries.

Enjoy this homemade version of the McDonald's Mac Burger sauce made with halal ingredients, adding a delicious touch to your homemade burgers!

McDonald's-Style McNuggets Recipe

Ingredients:

- 1 pound boneless chicken breasts
  - 1 cup all-purpose flour
  - 1 teaspoon paprika
  - 1 teaspoon garlic powder
  - 1 teaspoon onion powder
  - 1 teaspoon salt
  - 1/2 teaspoon black pepper
  - 1 egg
  - 1/2 cup milk
  - Vegetable oil for frying

Tools Required:

- Knife
  - Cutting board
  - Mixing bowls
  - Frying pan or deep fryer
  - Paper towels
  - Tongs or slotted spoon

Method:

Preparing the Chicken:

Chicken Cutting:

- Cut the chicken breasts into bite-sized pieces or nuggets.

Seasoned Coating:

- In a mixing bowl, combine flour, paprika, garlic powder, onion powder, salt, and black pepper. Mix the ingredients thoroughly.

Coating the Chicken:

- In another bowl, whisk together the egg and milk.

- Dip each piece of chicken into the egg mixture, allowing excess to drip off, then coat thoroughly in the seasoned flour mixture.

Frying the McNuggets:

Heating the Oil:

- Heat vegetable oil in a frying pan or deep fryer to around 350°F (175°C).

Frying Process:

- Carefully add the coated chicken pieces into the hot oil in batches. Fry for about 5-6 minutes until they turn golden brown and are fully cooked through.

Draining and Cooling:

- Use tongs or a slotted spoon to transfer the fried McNuggets to a plate lined with paper towels. This helps absorb excess oil and cools them down.

Serving:

Ready to Enjoy:

- Serve the McDonald's-style McNuggets hot with your favorite dipping sauce.

Additional Tips:

- For extra flavor, you can add additional spices or herbs to the flour mixture, such as a pinch of cayenne pepper for heat or a dash of dried herbs like thyme or oregano for added aroma.

● Experiment with different dipping sauces like barbecue, honey mustard, or sweet and sour for a variety of flavors.

Enjoy these homemade McNuggets made with halal ingredients, perfect as a snack or part of a meal!

McDonald's-Style Egg McMuffin Recipe

Ingredients:

- 1 English muffin
  - 1 large egg
  - 1 slice Canadian beef or cooked beef
  - 1 slice American cheese
  - Butter or cooking spray
  - Salt and pepper to taste

Tools Required:

- Skillet with lid or microwave
  - Non-stick frying pan or egg rings
  - Spatula

Method:

Cooking the Egg:

Pan Method:

- Heat a non-stick frying pan over medium heat. Lightly grease the pan or egg rings with butter or cooking spray.

- Crack the egg into the pan or egg ring. Pierce the yolk gently with a fork and sprinkle a pinch of salt and pepper over it.

- Cover the pan with a lid and cook for about 2-3 minutes until the egg white is set and the yolk is cooked to your preference.

Microwave Method:

- Grease a microwave-safe bowl or small dish with butter or cooking spray.

• Crack the egg into the bowl and pierce the yolk gently with a fork. Season with salt and pepper.

• Cover the bowl with a microwave-safe lid or plate and microwave on high for about 1-1.5 minutes until the egg white is set and the yolk reaches your desired doneness.

Assembling the McMuffin:

Toasting the English Muffin:

• Slice the English muffin in half and lightly toast both halves.

Layering Ingredients:

• Place the cooked Canadian beef or beef slice on the bottom half of the toasted muffin.

• Add the cooked egg on top of the beef.

• Place the slice of American cheese on the egg.

Completing the Sandwich:

• Top the sandwich with the other half of the toasted English muffin.

Serving:

Ready to Enjoy:

• Serve the McDonald's-style Egg McMuffin immediately.

Additional Tips:

• Customize your Egg McMuffin by adding ingredients like sliced tomatoes, avocado, or beef for extra flavor.

• If using egg rings, ensure they are well-greased to prevent the egg from sticking.

● Feel free to use a substitute for Canadian beef or beef if preferred.

Enjoy this homemade version of the McDonald's Egg McMuffin made with halal ingredients, perfect for a delicious breakfast!

McDonald's-Style McFlurry Recipe

Ingredients:

- Vanilla ice cream
  - Mix-ins (such as chocolate chips, Oreo cookies, M&M's, or fruit)

Tools Required:

- Blender or food processor
  - Mixing spoon or spatula
  - Serving cups or bowls

Method:

Preparing the McFlurry:

Softening the Ice Cream:

- Take a few scoops of vanilla ice cream from the container and let it sit at room temperature for a few minutes to slightly soften.

Crushing Mix-ins (if needed):

- If using ingredients like cookies or candies, crush them into smaller pieces. For example, crush Oreo cookies or chocolate candies into smaller chunks.

Blending the Ice Cream and Mix-ins:

- In a blender or food processor, add the softened vanilla ice cream.
- Add the crushed mix-ins of your choice into the blender.

Blending Process:

• Blend the ice cream and mix-ins together on low speed or pulse mode. Avoid over-blending; you want to maintain some texture and small pieces of the mix-ins.

Serving:

Portioning into Cups:

• Transfer the blended McFlurry mixture into serving cups or bowls.

Optional Toppings:

• You can add additional toppings like a dollop of whipped cream, chocolate syrup, or more crushed mix-ins on top if desired.

Additional Tips:

• Experiment with different mix-ins to create various flavors. Try combining different chocolates, candies, nuts, or fruits for unique McFlurry variations.

• Adjust the blending time according to your preference for the texture of the mix-ins in the McFlurry.

Enjoy this homemade version of the McDonald's McFlurry made with halal ingredients, providing a delightful and customizable frozen treat!

McDonald's-Style Filet-O-Fish Recipe

Ingredients:

- Fish fillets (such as cod, haddock, or pollock)
  - Breadcrumbs
  - 1 egg
  - Sliced cheese
  - Tartar sauce
  - burger buns

Tools Required:

- Frying pan or skillet
  - Cooking oil
  - Mixing bowl
  - Whisk or fork
  - Spatula

Method:

Preparing the Fish:

Coating the Fish:

- In a mixing bowl, beat the egg. Dip the fish fillets in the beaten egg, ensuring they are well coated.

- Coat the fish fillets in breadcrumbs, covering them completely.

Frying the Fish:

- Heat cooking oil in a frying pan or skillet over medium heat.

- Carefully place the breaded fish fillets into the hot oil and fry for approximately 3-4 minutes on each side, or until they are golden brown and cooked through.

Assembling the Sandwich:

Toasting the Buns:

- Lightly toast the burger buns in a separate pan or toaster.

Layering the Ingredients:

- Spread tartar sauce on the bottom half of each toasted bun.
- Place a slice of cheese on top of the tartar sauce.
- Add the fried fish fillet on top of the cheese.

Completing the Sandwich:

- Cover the fish fillet with the top half of the toasted bun.

Serving:

Ready to Enjoy:

- Serve the McDonald's-style Filet-O-Fish immediately.

Additional Tips:

- Ensure the fish filets are patted dry before coating them with egg and breadcrumbs to help the coating adhere better.
- Customize your Filet-O-Fish sandwich by adding lettuce or pickles for extra flavor and texture.

Enjoy this homemade version of the McDonald's Filet-O-Fish made with halal ingredients, offering a delicious sandwich option!

McDonald's-Style Apple Pie Recipe

Ingredients:

- Puff pastry sheets
  - Apples (peeled, cored, and diced)
  - Sugar
  - Cinnamon
  - Lemon juice
  - Cornstarch
  - Butter (optional)

Tools Required:

- Baking sheet
  - Parchment paper
  - Knife
  - Fork
  - Bowl
  - Pastry brush (optional)

Method:

Preparing the Apple Filling:

Prepping the Apples:

- Peel, core, and dice the apples into small pieces.

Mixing Ingredients:

- In a bowl, combine the diced apples with sugar, a dash of cinnamon, a squeeze of lemon juice, and a small amount of cornstarch. Mix well to coat the apples evenly.

Assembling the Apple Pie:

Cutting and Shaping Pastry:

- Cut the puff pastry sheets into squares or rectangles of equal size, suitable for making individual pies.

Placing Apple Filling:

- Spoon the prepared apple mixture onto one half of each pastry square.

Sealing and Crimping:

- Fold the other half of the pastry over the apple filling to create a pocket. Use a fork to press down and seal the edges firmly.

Optional Brushing (for shine):

- Optionally, lightly brush the tops of the pies with melted butter or egg wash using a pastry brush for a golden finish.

Baking the Pies:

Preparation and Baking:

- Preheat the oven to the specified temperature according to the puff pastry package instructions.

- Place the prepared apple pies on a baking sheet lined with parchment paper.

Baking Process:

- Bake the pies in the preheated oven according to the puff pastry package instructions or until they turn golden brown.

Serving:

Cooling and Enjoying:

- Allow the McDonald's-style apple pies to cool slightly before serving.

Additional Tips:

- Adjust the sweetness and cinnamon according to your taste preferences.
- These pies taste great when served warm, and you can pair them with a scoop of vanilla ice cream for a delightful treat.

Enjoy this homemade version of the McDonald's apple pie made with halal ingredients, perfect for a sweet and comforting dessert!

McDonald's-Style Strawberry Shake Recipe

Ingredients:

- Fresh or frozen strawberries
  - Vanilla ice cream
  - Milk
  - Sugar (optional)

Tools Required:

- Blender
  - Drinking glasses
  - Drinking straws

Method:

Preparing the Shake:

Prepping Strawberries:

- Wash and hull the strawberries if using fresh ones. If using frozen strawberries, thaw them slightly.

Blending Ingredients:

- In a blender, combine the strawberries, a few scoops of vanilla ice cream, a splash of milk, and sugar (if desired for extra sweetness).

Blending Process:

- Blend the ingredients until smooth and well combined. Add more milk if needed to reach the desired consistency.

Serving the Shake:

Pouring into Glasses:

• Pour the strawberry shake into drinking glasses.

Optional Garnish:

• Optionally, you can top the shakes with a dollop of whipped cream or a sliced strawberry for decoration.

Additional Tips:

• Adjust the sweetness by adding more or less sugar according to your taste preference.

• For a thicker shake, use more ice cream and fewer strawberries. For a lighter version, increase the amount of strawberries and reduce the ice cream.

Enjoy this homemade version of the McDonald's strawberry shake made with halal ingredients, providing a refreshing and delicious treat!

Hardee's-Style Thickburgers Recipe

Ingredients:

- Ground beef
  - burger buns
  - Salt
  - Black pepper
  - Cheese slices
  - Lettuce leaves
  - Tomato slices
  - Onion slices
  - Pickles
  - Condiments (ketchup, mustard, mayo)

Tools Required:

- Grill or frying pan
  - Spatula
  - Knife
  - Cutting board

Method:

Preparing the Patties:

Shaping Patties:

- Divide the ground beef into portions and shape them into burger patties, ensuring they're slightly larger than the burger buns.

Seasoning Patties:

- Sprinkle salt and black pepper on both sides of each patty for seasoning.

Cooking the Patties:

Grilling or Frying:

- Heat a grill or frying pan over medium-high heat.

- Place the seasoned patties onto the heated surface and cook for about 3-4 minutes on each side, or until they reach your preferred level of doneness.

Melting Cheese (Optional):

- Place cheese slices on top of the patties during the last minute of cooking to allow them to melt.

Assembling the Burger:

Preparing Buns:

- Lightly toast the burger buns on the grill or in a toaster.

Layering Ingredients:

- Place a cooked patty with or without melted cheese on the bottom half of the bun.

- Add lettuce leaves, tomato slices, onion slices, and pickles on top of the patty.

Adding Condiments:

- Spread condiments (ketchup, mustard, mayo) on the top half of the bun.

Completing the Burger:

- Place the top half of the bun over the assembled ingredients to complete the burger.

Serving:

Ready to Enjoy:

- Serve the Hardee's-style Thickburger immediately.

Additional Tips:

- Customize your Thickburger by adding beef, additional cheese, or other toppings you prefer.
- Ensure the patties are cooked thoroughly to your desired level of doneness before assembling the burger.

Enjoy this homemade version of the Hardee's Thickburger made with halal ingredients, providing a delicious and hearty meal!

Hardee's-Style Hand-Breaded Chicken Tenders Recipe

Ingredients:

- Chicken tenderloins or chicken breast strips
  - All-purpose flour
  - Eggs
  - Milk
  - Salt
  - Black pepper
  - Garlic powder
  - Cooking oil (for frying)

Tools Required:

- Mixing bowls
  - Frying pan or skillet
  - Tongs
  - Paper towels
  - Wire rack (optional)

Method:

Preparing the Chicken:

Seasoning Chicken:

- Pat dry the chicken tenderloins or breast strips with paper towels.

- Season the chicken with salt, black pepper, and garlic powder according to taste.

Breading Station:

- Prepare a breading station with three bowls: one with flour, one with beaten eggs and a splash of milk, and one empty for the coated chicken.

Breading the Chicken:

Coating Chicken:

- Dip each piece of chicken first in the flour, coating it evenly.

- Then dip the floured chicken into the egg mixture, allowing excess to drip off.

- Coat the chicken again in the flour for a second layer, pressing gently to adhere.

Frying the Chicken:

Heating Oil:

- Heat cooking oil in a frying pan or skillet over medium-high heat until it reaches about 350-375°F (175-190°C).

Frying Process:

- Carefully place the breaded chicken tenders into the hot oil using tongs.

- Fry the chicken for about 4-5 minutes per side, or until golden brown and fully cooked.

Draining Excess Oil:

- Once cooked, remove the chicken tenders from the oil and place them on a wire rack or paper towels to drain excess oil.

Serving:

Ready to Enjoy:

- Serve the Hardee's-style Hand-Breaded Chicken Tenders hot, alongside your favorite dipping sauce.

Additional Tips:

- Ensure the oil is at the right temperature before frying to achieve a crispy coating without absorbing excess oil.

- You can adjust the seasoning according to your taste preferences by adding herbs or spices to the flour mixture.

Enjoy these homemade Hardee's-style Hand-Breaded Chicken Tenders made with halal ingredients for a delightful meal or snack!

Hardee's-Style Famous Star Burger Recipe

Ingredients:

- Ground beef
  - burger buns
  - Salt
  - Black pepper
  - American cheese slices
  - Lettuce leaves
  - Tomato slices
  - Onion slices
  - Pickles
  - Ketchup
  - Mustard
  - Mayonnaise

Tools Required:

- Grill or frying pan
  - Spatula
  - Knife
  - Cutting board

Method:

Preparing the Patties:

Shaping Patties:

- Divide the ground beef into portions and shape them into burger patties of equal size, slightly larger than the burger buns.

Seasoning Patties:

- Sprinkle salt and black pepper on both sides of each patty for seasoning.

Cooking the Patties:

Grilling or Frying:

- Heat a grill or frying pan over medium-high heat.

- Place the seasoned patties onto the heated surface and cook for about 3-4 minutes on each side, or until they reach your preferred level of doneness.

Assembling the Burger:

Preparing Buns:

- Lightly toast the burger buns on the grill or in a toaster.

Layering Ingredients:

- Place a cooked patty on the bottom half of the bun.

- Add a slice of American cheese on top of the patty.

- Add lettuce leaves, tomato slices, onion slices, and pickles on top of the cheese.

Adding Condiments:

- Spread ketchup, mustard, and mayonnaise on the top half of the bun.

Completing the Burger:

- Place the top half of the bun over the assembled ingredients to complete the burger.

Serving:

Ready to Enjoy:

- Serve the Hardee's-style Famous Star Burger immediately.

Additional Tips:

- Customize your Famous Star Burger with additional toppings like beef or extra cheese.
- Ensure the patties are cooked thoroughly to your desired level of doneness before assembling the burger.

Enjoy this homemade version of the Hardee's Famous Star Burger made with halal ingredients for a flavorful and satisfying meal!

Hardee's-Style Chicken Fillet Sandwich Recipe

Ingredients:

- Chicken breast fillets
  - All-purpose flour
  - Eggs
  - Milk
  - Salt
  - Black pepper
  - Garlic powder
  - burger buns
  - Lettuce leaves
  - Tomato slices
  - Mayonnaise
  - Pickles (optional)

Tools Required:

- Frying pan or skillet
  - Mixing bowls
  - Whisk or fork
  - Tongs
  - Paper towels

Method:

Preparing the Chicken:

Prepping Chicken Fillets:

- Pat dry the chicken breast fillets using paper towels.

Seasoning Chicken:

- Season the chicken fillets with salt, black pepper, and garlic powder according to taste.

Breading the Chicken:

Coating Chicken:

- Prepare a breading station with three bowls: one with flour, one with beaten eggs and a splash of milk, and one empty for the coated chicken.

Dipping and Coating:

- Dip each chicken fillet first in the flour, coating it evenly.

- Then dip the floured chicken into the egg mixture, allowing excess to drip off.

- Coat the chicken again in the flour for a second layer, pressing gently to adhere.

Cooking the Chicken:

Heating Oil:

- Heat oil in a frying pan or skillet over medium-high heat until it reaches about 350°F (175°C).

Frying Process:

- Carefully place the breaded chicken fillets into the hot oil using tongs.

- Fry the chicken for about 4-5 minutes per side, or until golden brown and fully cooked.

Draining Excess Oil:

- Once cooked, remove the chicken fillets from the oil and place them on paper towels to drain excess oil.

Assembling the Sandwich:

Preparing Buns:

- Lightly toast the burger buns.

Layering Ingredients:

- Spread mayonnaise on both halves of the buns.

- Place a fried chicken fillet on the bottom half of the bun.

- Add lettuce leaves, tomato slices, and pickles (if using) on top of the chicken.

Completing the Sandwich:

- Place the top half of the bun over the assembled ingredients to complete the sandwich.

Serving:

Ready to Enjoy:

- Serve the Hardee's-style Chicken Fillet Sandwich immediately.

Additional Tips:

- Adjust the seasoning by adding herbs or spices to the flour mixture for extra flavor.
- Ensure the oil is at the right temperature before frying to achieve a crispy coating without absorbing excess oil.

Enjoy this homemade version of the Hardee's Chicken Fillet Sandwich made with halal ingredients for a delicious meal!

Hardee's-Style Fried Chicken Recipe

Ingredients:

- Chicken pieces (drumsticks, thighs, or breasts)
  - All-purpose flour
  - Eggs
  - Milk
  - Salt
  - Black pepper
  - Garlic powder
  - Paprika (optional)
  - Cooking oil

Tools Required:

- Frying pan or skillet
  - Mixing bowls
  - Whisk or fork
  - Tongs
  - Paper towels

Method:

Preparing the Chicken:

Cleaning Chicken:

- Rinse the chicken pieces under cold water and pat them dry with paper towels.

Seasoning Chicken:

- Season the chicken pieces with salt, black pepper, garlic powder, and paprika (if using) according to taste.

Coating the Chicken:

Breading Station:

- Prepare a breading station with three bowls: one with flour, one with beaten eggs and a splash of milk, and one empty for the coated chicken.

Coating Process:

- Dip each piece of chicken first in the flour, coating it evenly.

- Then dip the floured chicken into the egg mixture, allowing excess to drip off.

- Coat the chicken again in the flour for a second layer, pressing gently to adhere.

Frying the Chicken:

Heating Oil:

- Heat oil in a frying pan or skillet over medium-high heat until it reaches about 350°F (175°C).

Frying Process:

- Carefully place the breaded chicken pieces into the hot oil using tongs.

- Fry the chicken for about 12-15 minutes, turning occasionally, until golden brown and fully cooked.

Draining Excess Oil:

- Once cooked, remove the fried chicken pieces from the oil and place them on paper towels to drain excess oil.

Serving:

Ready to Enjoy:

- Serve the Hardee's-style Fried Chicken hot as a delightful meal or snack.

Additional Tips:

- Adjust the seasoning by adding herbs or spices to the flour mixture for added flavor.
- Use a thermometer to ensure the oil reaches the correct temperature for crispy and properly cooked chicken.

Enjoy this homemade version of the Hardee's Fried Chicken made with halal ingredients for a delicious and crispy treat!

Hardee's-Style Hand-Breaded Chicken Sandwich Recipe

Ingredients:

- Chicken breast fillets
  - All-purpose flour
  - Eggs
  - Milk
  - Salt
  - Black pepper
  - Garlic powder
  - burger buns
  - Lettuce leaves
  - Tomato slices
  - Mayonnaise
  - Pickles (optional)

Tools Required:

- Frying pan or skillet
  - Mixing bowls
  - Whisk or fork
  - Tongs
  - Paper towels

Method:

Preparing the Chicken:

Prepping Chicken Fillets:

- Pat dry the chicken breast fillets using paper towels.

Seasoning Chicken:

- Season the chicken fillets with salt, black pepper, and garlic powder according to taste.

Breading the Chicken:

Coating Chicken:

- Prepare a breading station with three bowls: one with flour, one with beaten eggs and a splash of milk, and one empty for the coated chicken.

Dipping and Coating:

- Dip each chicken fillet first in the flour, coating it evenly.

- Then dip the floured chicken into the egg mixture, allowing excess to drip off.

- Coat the chicken again in the flour for a second layer, pressing gently to adhere.

Cooking the Chicken:

Heating Oil:

- Heat oil in a frying pan or skillet over medium-high heat until it reaches about 350°F (175°C).

Frying Process:

- Carefully place the breaded chicken fillets into the hot oil using tongs.

- Fry the chicken for about 4-5 minutes per side, or until golden brown and fully cooked.

Draining Excess Oil:

- Once cooked, remove the chicken fillets from the oil and place them on paper towels to drain excess oil.

Assembling the Sandwich:

Preparing Buns:

- Lightly toast the burger buns.

Layering Ingredients:

- Spread mayonnaise on both halves of the buns.

- Place a fried chicken fillet on the bottom half of the bun.

- Add lettuce leaves, tomato slices, and pickles (if using) on top of the chicken.

Completing the Sandwich:

- Place the top half of the bun over the assembled ingredients to complete the sandwich.

Serving:

Ready to Enjoy:

- Serve the Hardee's-style Hand-Breaded Chicken Sandwich immediately.

Additional Tips:

- Adjust the seasoning by adding herbs or spices to the flour mixture for extra flavor.
- Ensure the oil is at the right temperature before frying to achieve a crispy coating without absorbing excess oil.

Enjoy this homemade version of the Hardee's Hand-Breaded Chicken Sandwich made with halal ingredients for a flavorful meal!

Hardee's-Style Onion Rings Recipe

Ingredients:

- Onions
    - All-purpose flour
    - Cornmeal
    - Baking powder
    - Salt
    - Black pepper
    - Milk
    - Cooking oil

Tools Required:

- Mixing bowls
    - Deep frying pan or skillet
    - Tongs
    - Paper towels

Method:

Preparing the Onions:

Slicing Onions:

- Peel the onions and slice them into thick rings. Separate the rings and set them aside.

Making the Batter:

Mixing Dry Ingredients:

- In a mixing bowl, combine all-purpose flour, cornmeal, baking powder, salt, and black pepper.

Adding Milk:

- Gradually pour in milk while stirring to create a smooth and thick batter. Adjust milk quantity if needed for desired consistency.

Frying the Onion Rings:

Heating Oil:

- Heat cooking oil in a deep frying pan or skillet over medium-high heat.

Coating Onion Rings:

- Dip each onion ring into the batter, ensuring it's completely coated.

Frying Process:

- Carefully place the coated onion rings into the hot oil using tongs, a few at a time.

- Fry the onion rings for about 2-3 minutes per side, or until they turn golden brown and crispy.

Draining Excess Oil:

- Once fried, remove the onion rings from the oil and place them on paper towels to absorb excess oil.

Serving:

Ready to Enjoy:

- Serve the Hardee's-style Onion Rings hot as a delicious side dish or snack.

Additional Tips:

● Ensure the oil is hot enough before frying to prevent the onion rings from becoming oily.

● Work in batches while frying to avoid overcrowding the pan, which can lower the oil temperature and affect crispness.

Enjoy this homemade version of Hardee's Onion Rings made with halal ingredients for a crispy and flavorful treat!

Hardee's-Style Hash Rounds Recipe

Ingredients:

- Potatoes
  - Salt
  - Black pepper
  - Garlic powder
  - Onion powder
  - Cooking oil

Tools Required:

- Mixing bowl
  - Baking sheet
  - Spatula

Method:

Preparing the Potatoes:

Cleaning Potatoes:

- Wash and scrub the potatoes thoroughly to remove any dirt.

Grating Potatoes:

- Using a grater, grate the potatoes into a mixing bowl.

Seasoning the Hash Rounds:

Seasoning Mixture:

- In the bowl with grated potatoes, add salt, black pepper, garlic powder, and onion powder according to taste.

Mixing Ingredients:

● Mix the seasoning thoroughly with the grated potatoes until well combined.

Shaping the Hash Rounds:

Forming Rounds:

● Take a portion of the seasoned potato mixture and shape it into small, flat rounds using your hands. Press firmly to compact them.

Cooking the Hash Rounds:

Preheating Oven:

● Preheat the oven to 400°F (200°C) and line a baking sheet with parchment paper.

Baking Process:

● Place the shaped hash rounds onto the prepared baking sheet in a single layer.

Baking Time:

● Bake the hash rounds in the preheated oven for approximately 20-25 minutes, flipping them halfway through, until they turn golden brown and crispy.

Serving:

Ready to Enjoy:

● Serve the Hardee's-style Hash Rounds hot as a tasty side dish or breakfast addition.

Additional Tips:

● Ensure the grated potatoes are well-drained to prevent excess moisture while shaping the hash rounds.

● Adjust seasoning according to personal taste preferences for added flavor.

Enjoy making these homemade Hardee's Hash Rounds with halal ingredients for a delightful and crispy treat!

Hardee's-Style Loaded Omelet Biscuit Recipe

Ingredients:

- Biscuits (store-bought or homemade)
  - Eggs
  - Breakfast sausage or halal meat alternative
  - Shredded cheese
  - Salt
  - Black pepper
  - Cooking oil or butter
  - Optional toppings: chopped onions, bell peppers, or tomatoes

Tools Required:

- Frying pan or skillet
  - Mixing bowl
  - Spatula

Method:

Preparing the Ingredients:

Cooking Breakfast Sausage:

- If using breakfast sausage, cook it in a frying pan over medium heat until browned. Drain excess fat and set it aside.

Optional Toppings:

- Chop any additional toppings like onions, bell peppers, or tomatoes if desired.

Making the Omelet:

Whisking Eggs:

● Crack the eggs into a mixing bowl, add a pinch of salt and black pepper, and whisk until well beaten.

Cooking Eggs:

● Heat a little oil or butter in the frying pan over medium-low heat.

● Pour the beaten eggs into the pan and let them cook until the edges start to set.

Adding Toppings:

● Sprinkle the cooked sausage and any optional toppings evenly over the partially cooked eggs.

Folding Omelet:

● Once the eggs are mostly set but still slightly runny on top, fold one side of the omelet over the toppings to create a half-moon shape.

Adding Cheese:

● Sprinkle shredded cheese over the top of the omelet and cover the pan to let the cheese melt.

Preparing the Biscuits:

Heating Biscuits:

● Warm the biscuits in the oven according to package instructions or prepare homemade biscuits if using those.

Assembling the Loaded Omelet Biscuit:

Placing Omelet on Biscuits:

● Open each biscuit and place a portion of the loaded omelet inside.

Serving:

Ready to Enjoy:

- Serve the Hardee's-style Loaded Omelet Biscuits warm as a hearty and satisfying breakfast option.

Additional Tips:

- Customize the omelet with preferred toppings and cheese variations for added flavor.
- Ensure the omelet is cooked through before serving to guarantee a delicious and safe breakfast experience.

Enjoy creating this homemade Hardee's Loaded Omelet Biscuit with halal ingredients for a delightful morning treat!

Hardee's-Style Monster Biscuit Recipe

Ingredients:

- Biscuits (store-bought or homemade)
    - Breakfast sausage or halal meat alternative
    - Sliced beef
    - beef strips
    - Eggs
    - American cheese slices
    - Salt
    - Black pepper
    - Cooking oil or butter

Tools Required:

- Frying pan or skillet
    - Baking sheet
    - Mixing bowl
    - Spatula

Method:

Preparing the Ingredients:

Cooking Breakfast Sausage:

- If using breakfast sausage, cook it in a frying pan over medium heat until browned. Drain excess fat and set it aside.

Cooking beef and beef:

- Cook beef strips in the oven or frying pan until crispy. Cook sliced beef in a separate pan until lightly browned. Set them aside.

Whisking Eggs:

- Crack eggs into a mixing bowl, add a pinch of salt and black pepper, and whisk until well beaten.

Making the Monster Biscuit:

Cooking Eggs:

- Heat a little oil or butter in a frying pan over medium-low heat.

- Pour the beaten eggs into the pan and let them cook until the edges start to set.

Adding Sausage and Cheese:

- Sprinkle cooked sausage over the partially cooked eggs. Place American cheese slices on top to melt.

Assembling the Biscuits:

- Warm the biscuits in the oven according to package instructions or prepare homemade biscuits if using those.

- Split the biscuits in half and layer the cooked egg, sausage, and cheese mixture onto the bottom half.

Adding beef and beef:

- Add a layer of cooked beef slices on top of the egg mixture. Then place crispy beef strips on top of the beef.

Completing the Sandwich:

- Top with the other half of the biscuit to form a sandwich.

Serving:

Ready to Enjoy:

● Serve the Hardee's-style Monster Biscuit warm as a substantial breakfast or brunch option.

Additional Tips:

● Customize the Monster Biscuit with preferred meats or additional ingredients for personal taste preferences.

● Ensure all components are cooked thoroughly before assembling for a delightful breakfast experience.

Enjoy crafting this homemade Hardee's Monster Biscuit with halal ingredients for a hearty morning meal!

Hardee's-Style French Toast Dips Recipe

Ingredients:

- Bread slices (white or whole wheat)
  - Eggs
  - Milk
  - Vanilla extract
  - Cinnamon powder
  - Butter or cooking oil
  - Maple syrup or honey (optional)

Tools Required:

- Mixing bowl
  - Whisk
  - Frying pan or griddle
  - Spatula

Method:

Preparing the French Toast Mixture:

Whisking Eggs:

- Crack eggs into a mixing bowl. Add a splash of milk, a few drops of vanilla extract, and a pinch of cinnamon powder. Whisk the mixture until well combined.

Dipping the Bread:

Soaking Bread Slices:

- Heat a frying pan or griddle over medium heat and add a little butter or oil to coat the surface.

- Dip each bread slice into the egg mixture, ensuring both sides are well soaked but not overly saturated.

Cooking the French Toast:

Cooking Bread Slices:

- Place the dipped bread slices onto the preheated pan or griddle.

- Cook each side for approximately 2-3 minutes or until golden brown and cooked through.

Serving:

Ready to Enjoy:

- Serve the Hardee's-style French Toast Dips warm and crispy as a delightful breakfast or brunch option.

Optional Toppings:

- Drizzle maple syrup or honey over the French toast dips for added sweetness, if desired.

Additional Tips:

- Adjust the amount of cinnamon or vanilla extract according to personal taste preferences.
- Serve with fresh fruits, whipped cream, or your preferred toppings for a delightful twist.

Enjoy making these homemade Hardee's-style French Toast Dips with halal ingredients for a delightful morning treat!

Burger King Whopper Recipe

Ingredients:

- Ground beef
    - burger buns
    - Lettuce
    - Tomato slices
    - Onion slices
    - Pickles
    - American cheese slices
    - Ketchup
    - Mayonnaise
    - Mustard
    - Salt
    - Black pepper
    - Cooking oil

Tools Required:

- Frying pan or grill
    - Spatula
    - Knife and cutting board

Method:

Preparing the Ingredients:

Shaping Patties:

- Divide the ground beef into portions and shape them into round patties. Season with salt and pepper on both sides.

Prepping Vegetables:

- Wash and slice the lettuce, tomato, onion, and pickles.

Cooking the Patties:

Cooking Beef Patties:

- Heat a frying pan or grill over medium-high heat and add a bit of oil.

- Place the patties onto the hot surface and cook for about 3-4 minutes on each side or until desired doneness.

- In the last minute of cooking, add a slice of cheese on top of each patty and allow it to melt.

Assembling the Whopper:

Toasting Buns:

- Lightly toast the burger buns in the pan or on the grill until they're warm and slightly golden.

Building the Burger:

- On the bottom half of the bun, spread some ketchup, mayonnaise, and mustard.

- Layer the lettuce, tomato slices, onion slices, and pickles on top of the sauces.

- Place the cooked beef patty with melted cheese on top of the veggies.

- Cover the patty with the top half of the bun.

Serving:

Ready to Enjoy:

- Serve your homemade Whopper with homemade fries or side salad for a delightful meal!

Additional Tips:

• Experiment with the toppings and condiments to suit personal preferences.

• Ensure the beef patties are cooked thoroughly before assembling the burger.

Enjoy crafting your own Whopper at home with halal ingredients for a satisfying meal!

Burger King Cheeseburger Recipe

Ingredients:

- Ground beef
  - burger buns
  - Sliced cheese (American or Cheddar)
  - Lettuce
  - Tomato slices
  - Onion slices
  - Pickles
  - Ketchup
  - Mustard
  - Salt
  - Black pepper
  - Cooking oil

Tools Required:

- Frying pan or grill
  - Spatula
  - Knife and cutting board

Method:

Preparing the Ingredients:

Shaping Patties:

- Divide the ground beef into portions and shape them into round patties. Season with salt and pepper on both sides.

Prepping Vegetables:

- Wash and slice the lettuce, tomato, onion, and pickles.

Cooking the Patties:

Cooking Beef Patties:

- Heat a frying pan or grill over medium-high heat and add a bit of oil.

- Place the patties onto the hot surface and cook for about 3-4 minutes on each side or until desired doneness.

Assembling the Cheeseburger:

Melting Cheese:

- In the last minute of cooking, place a slice of cheese on top of each patty and allow it to melt.

Building the Burger:

- On the bottom half of the bun, spread some ketchup and mustard.

- Layer the lettuce, tomato slices, onion slices, and pickles on top of the sauces.

- Place the cooked beef patty with melted cheese on top of the veggies.

- Cover the patty with the top half of the bun.

Serving:

Ready to Enjoy:

- Serve your homemade cheeseburger with a side of fries or salad for a delightful meal!

Additional Tips:

● Customize your cheeseburger with additional toppings like sautéed mushrooms, or different types of cheese for a flavorful twist.

● Ensure the beef patties are thoroughly cooked before assembling the burger.

Enjoy creating your own delicious cheeseburgers at home using halal ingredients!

Burger King Chicken Fries Recipe

Ingredients:

- Chicken breast (boneless, skinless)
  - Flour
  - Cornstarch
  - Eggs
  - Salt
  - Black pepper
  - Garlic powder
  - Onion powder
  - Paprika
  - Cooking oil

Tools Required:

- Cutting board
  - Knife
  - Bowls for dredging
  - Frying pan
  - Tongs

Method:

Preparing the Chicken:

Cutting Chicken Strips:

- Cut the chicken breast into strips resembling French fries.

Dredging the Chicken:

Setting Up Dredging Stations:

- In one bowl, mix flour, cornstarch, salt, black pepper, garlic powder, onion powder, and paprika.

- In another bowl, beat the eggs.

Coating the Chicken:

- Dip each chicken strip into the flour mixture, ensuring it's evenly coated.

- Next, dip the coated strip into the beaten eggs, then back into the flour mixture for a double coating.

Cooking the Chicken Fries:

Heating Oil:

- Heat cooking oil in a frying pan over medium-high heat.

Frying the Chicken:

- Carefully place the coated chicken strips into the hot oil, a few at a time.

- Fry until they turn golden brown and are cooked through, usually about 3-4 minutes per side.

Draining Excess Oil:

- Once done, remove the chicken fries from the oil and place them on a paper towel-lined plate to drain off excess oil.

Serving:

Ready to Enjoy:

- Serve your homemade chicken fries with your favorite dipping sauce!

Additional Tips:

● For extra flavor, marinate the chicken strips in buttermilk or a seasoned brine before coating and frying.

● Experiment with different spices and seasonings to suit your taste preferences.

Enjoy creating your own crispy chicken fries at home using halal ingredients!

Burger King-style Chicken Sandwich Recipe

Ingredients:

- 2 boneless, skinless halal chicken breasts
  - 1 cup buttermilk
  - 1 cup all-purpose flour
  - 1 teaspoon paprika
  - 1 teaspoon garlic powder
  - 1 teaspoon onion powder
  - 1 teaspoon salt
  - 1 teaspoon black pepper
  - Vegetable oil for frying
  - 4 burger buns
  - 4 lettuce leaves
  - 4 tomato slices
  - 4 slices halal cheese (optional)
  - Mayonnaise
  - Pickles (optional)

Tools Required:

- Mixing bowls
  - Plastic wrap
  - Frying pan
  - Tongs
  - Paper towels
  - Cooking thermometer (optional)

Method:

1. Prep the Chicken:

Place the chicken breasts between two sheets of plastic wrap.

Use a meat mallet or rolling pin to gently pound the chicken to an even thickness, about half an inch thick.

2. Marinate:

In a mixing bowl, pour the buttermilk.

Add the pounded chicken breasts to the bowl, ensuring they are fully submerged.

Cover the bowl with plastic wrap and refrigerate for at least 30 minutes or up to 4 hours. This helps tenderize the chicken.

3. Prepare the Coating:

In another bowl, mix the flour, paprika, garlic powder, onion powder, salt, and black pepper.

Take out the marinated chicken from the buttermilk and let excess buttermilk drip off.

4. Coat the Chicken:

Dredge the chicken breasts in the seasoned flour mixture, making sure they are evenly coated.

Shake off any excess flour.

5. Fry the Chicken:

Heat vegetable oil in a frying pan over medium-high heat.

Once the oil is hot (around 350°F/175°C), carefully add the chicken breasts.

Fry for about 5-6 minutes per side, or until golden brown and cooked through.

Use a cooking thermometer to ensure the internal temperature reaches 165°F (74°C).

Place the fried chicken on a paper towel-lined plate to drain excess oil.

6. Assemble the Sandwiches:

Toast the burger buns lightly.

Spread mayonnaise on the bottom half of each bun.

Place a lettuce leaf on top of the mayo.

Add a fried chicken breast on each bun.

Optionally, add a slice of cheese on top of the hot chicken to melt slightly.

Top with a tomato slice and pickles, if desired.

Cover with the top half of the bun.

Additional Tips:

● For extra flavor, consider adding spices like cayenne pepper or smoked paprika to the flour mixture.

● If you prefer a spicier sandwich, you can incorporate hot sauce or chili powder into the buttermilk marinade.

● Ensure the oil temperature is right; too hot, and the chicken will burn, too cold, and it will become greasy.

● Don't overcrowd the frying pan to maintain the oil temperature and ensure even cooking.

Enjoy your homemade Burger King-style halal chicken sandwiches!

Burger King-style Veggie Burger Recipe

Ingredients:

- 1 can (15 ounces) chickpeas, drained and rinsed
  - 1/2 cup breadcrumbs
  - 1 small onion, finely chopped
  - 1 small carrot, grated
  - 1/2 cup cooked and mashed potatoes
  - 1 teaspoon garlic powder
  - 1 teaspoon cumin powder
  - 1 teaspoon paprika
  - Salt and pepper to taste
  - Vegetable oil for frying
  - Burger buns
  - Lettuce leaves
  - Tomato slices
  - Pickles
  - Mayonnaise
  - Ketchup

Tools Required:

- Mixing bowl
  - Potato masher or fork
  - Frying pan
  - Spatula
  - Paper towels

Method:

1. Prepare the Veggie Patty Mixture:

In a mixing bowl, mash the chickpeas using a potato masher or fork until partially mashed.

Add breadcrumbs, chopped onion, grated carrot, mashed potatoes, garlic powder, cumin powder, paprika, salt, and pepper.

Mix all the ingredients thoroughly until well combined.

2. Form Veggie Patties:

Take a handful of the mixture and shape it into a patty with your hands.

Ensure the patties are compacted well to prevent them from falling apart during cooking.

Repeat the process until all the mixture is used, making patties of desired size.

3. Cook the Veggie Patties:

Heat some vegetable oil in a frying pan over medium heat.

Once the oil is hot, carefully place the veggie patties in the pan.

Cook for about 4-5 minutes on each side, or until they are golden brown and crispy.

Use a spatula to flip them gently to avoid breaking.

4. Assemble the Burger:

Toast the burger buns lightly.

Spread mayonnaise and ketchup on the bottom half of each bun.

Place a lettuce leaf on top of the sauce.

Add a veggie patty onto the lettuce.

Top with tomato slices and pickles, if desired.

Cover with the top half of the bun.

Additional Tips:

• Experiment with additional spices like chili powder or herbs like parsley or cilantro to enhance the flavor of the patties.

• Ensure the veggie patties are cooked through but not overcooked to maintain their moisture and texture.

● You can also bake the patties in the oven for a healthier option. Preheat the oven to 375°F (190°C) and bake for about 15-20 minutes, flipping halfway through.

Enjoy your homemade BK-style halal veggie burgers!

Burger King-style Big Fish Sandwich Recipe

Ingredients:

- 2 fillets of halal white fish (such as cod or haddock)
  - 1 cup all-purpose flour
  - 1 teaspoon paprika
  - 1 teaspoon garlic powder
  - 1 teaspoon onion powder
  - 1 teaspoon salt
  - 1 teaspoon black pepper
  - Vegetable oil for frying
  - 4 burger buns
  - Lettuce leaves
  - Tomato slices
  - Tartar sauce (store-bought or homemade)

Tools Required:

- Mixing bowls
  - Frying pan
  - Tongs
  - Paper towels

Method:

1. Prepare the Fish Fillets:

Rinse the fish fillets under cold water and pat them dry with paper towels.
Cut the fillets, if needed, to fit the size of the burger buns.

2. Prepare the Coating:

In a mixing bowl, combine the all-purpose flour, paprika, garlic powder, onion powder, salt, and black pepper.
Mix the ingredients thoroughly to create the seasoned flour mixture.

3. Coat the Fish:

Heat vegetable oil in a frying pan over medium-high heat.

Coat each fish fillet evenly with the seasoned flour mixture, shaking off any excess.

4. Fry the Fish:

Once the oil is hot, carefully add the coated fish fillets to the pan.

Fry for about 3-4 minutes per side or until the fish is golden brown and cooked through.

Use tongs to carefully flip the fillets to ensure even cooking.

Place the fried fish on a paper towel-lined plate to drain excess oil.

5. Assemble the Sandwiches:

Toast the burger buns lightly.

Spread tartar sauce on the bottom half of each bun.

Place a lettuce leaf on top of the sauce.

Add a fried fish fillet onto the lettuce.

Top with tomato slices.

Cover with the top half of the bun.

Additional Tips:

• For a crispier coating, you can double coat the fish by dipping it in beaten egg before dredging it in the seasoned flour mixture.

• Experiment with adding a dash of lemon juice or vinegar to the tartar sauce for a tangier flavor.

• Ensure the oil is at the right temperature before frying the fish to achieve a crispy texture without absorbing excess oil.

• Serve the sandwiches immediately to enjoy the fish at its best texture and flavor.

Enjoy your homemade halal Big Fish Sandwich!

Burger King-style Tendercrisp Chicken Sandwich Recipe

Ingredients:

- 2 boneless, skinless halal chicken breasts
  - 1 cup buttermilk
  - 1 cup all-purpose flour
  - 1 teaspoon paprika
  - 1 teaspoon garlic powder
  - 1 teaspoon onion powder
  - 1 teaspoon salt
  - 1 teaspoon black pepper
  - Vegetable oil for frying
  - 4 burger buns
  - Lettuce leaves
  - Tomato slices
  - Mayonnaise
  - Pickles (optional)

Tools Required:

- Mixing bowls
  - Plastic wrap
  - Frying pan
  - Tongs
  - Paper towels

Method:

1. Prep the Chicken:

Lay the chicken breasts between plastic wrap.

Gently pound them with a meat mallet or rolling pin to an even thickness (about 1/2 inch).

2. Marinate the Chicken:

Pour the buttermilk into a mixing bowl.

Submerge the pounded chicken breasts in the buttermilk.

Cover the bowl with plastic wrap and refrigerate for at least 30 minutes or up to 4 hours.

3. Prepare the Coating:

In a separate bowl, mix the flour, paprika, garlic powder, onion powder, salt, and black pepper.

Take the marinated chicken out of the buttermilk and let excess liquid drip off.

4. Coat the Chicken:

Dredge the chicken breasts in the seasoned flour mixture until evenly coated.

Shake off any excess flour.

5. Fry the Chicken:

Heat vegetable oil in a frying pan over medium-high heat.

Once the oil is hot (around 350°F/175°C), carefully add the chicken breasts.

Fry for about 5-6 minutes per side or until golden brown and fully cooked.

Use tongs to flip the chicken for even frying.

Place the fried chicken on a paper towel-lined plate to drain excess oil.

6. Assemble the Sandwiches:

Lightly toast the burger buns.

Spread mayonnaise on the bottom half of each bun.

Place a lettuce leaf on the mayo.

Add a fried chicken breast on each bun.

Optionally, top with tomato slices and pickles.

Cover with the top half of the bun.

Additional Tips:

● For an extra kick, add spices like cayenne pepper or hot sauce to the seasoned flour mixture.

● Ensure the oil is at the right temperature before frying to achieve a crispy coating without making the chicken greasy.

● Don't overcrowd the frying pan; fry the chicken in batches if needed for even cooking.

Enjoy your homemade Halal Tendercrisp Chicken Sandwich!

Burger King-style Chicken Nuggets Recipe

Ingredients:

- 2 boneless, skinless halal chicken breasts
  - 1 cup all-purpose flour
  - 2 eggs
  - 1 cup breadcrumbs
  - 1 teaspoon paprika
  - 1 teaspoon garlic powder
  - 1 teaspoon onion powder
  - 1 teaspoon salt
  - 1 teaspoon black pepper
  - Vegetable oil for frying
  - Ketchup or your favorite dipping sauce

Tools Required:

- Cutting board
  - Knife
  - Bowls (for flour, beaten eggs, and breadcrumbs)
  - Frying pan
  - Tongs
  - Paper towels

Method:

1. Prepare the Chicken:

Trim any excess fat from the chicken breasts.

Cut the chicken into bite-sized pieces or nugget shapes.

2. Set Up Coating Stations:

In one bowl, mix the flour, paprika, garlic powder, onion powder, salt, and black pepper.

Crack the eggs into another bowl and beat them well.
Pour the breadcrumbs into a third bowl.

3. Coat the Chicken:

Take a piece of chicken and coat it thoroughly in the seasoned flour mixture.
Dip the coated chicken into the beaten eggs, ensuring it's fully covered.
Finally, coat the chicken in breadcrumbs, pressing gently to adhere.

4. Fry the Nuggets:

Heat vegetable oil in a frying pan over medium-high heat.
Once the oil is hot (around 350°F/175°C), carefully add the coated chicken nuggets.
Fry for about 3-4 minutes, turning occasionally, until they turn golden brown and are fully cooked.
Use tongs to transfer the cooked nuggets onto a plate lined with paper towels to absorb excess oil.

5. Serve:

Let the nuggets cool for a minute or two.
Serve them with your favorite dipping sauce, such as ketchup, barbecue sauce, or honey mustard.

Additional Tips:

● Ensure the oil is hot enough before frying to achieve crispy nuggets without absorbing excess oil.
● Don't overcrowd the frying pan; fry the nuggets in batches if needed for even cooking.
● For extra flavor, you can add additional spices like chili powder or Italian seasoning to the breadcrumbs or flour mixture.
Enjoy your homemade Halal Chicken Nuggets!

Burger King-style Onion Rings Recipe

Ingredients:

- 2 large onions
  - 1 cup all-purpose flour
  - 1 teaspoon paprika
  - 1 teaspoon garlic powder
  - 1 teaspoon salt
  - 1 teaspoon black pepper
  - 1 cup buttermilk
  - Vegetable oil for frying

Tools Required:

- Cutting board
  - Knife
  - Mixing bowls
  - Frying pan
  - Tongs
  - Paper towels

Method:

1. Prep the Onions:

Peel the onions and slice them into rings, about 1/2 inch thick.
Separate the rings and set them aside.

2. Prepare the Coating:

In a mixing bowl, combine the flour, paprika, garlic powder, salt, and black pepper.
Mix the ingredints well to create the seasoned flour mixture.

3. Coat the Onion Rings:

Dip an onion ring into the buttermilk, ensuring it's fully coated.

Coat the ring in the seasoned flour mixture, making sure it's evenly coated.

Repeat this process for all the onion rings, setting them aside on a plate.

4. Fry the Onion Rings:

Heat vegetable oil in a frying pan over medium-high heat.

Once the oil is hot (around 350°F/175°C), carefully add the coated onion rings in batches.

Fry for about 2-3 minutes per batch or until they turn golden brown and crispy.

Use tongs to transfer the fried onion rings to a plate lined with paper towels to remove excess oil.

5. Serve:

Let the onion rings cool for a minute before serving.

Enjoy them as a delicious side dish or snack!

Additional Tips:

• Ensure the oil is at the right temperature before frying to achieve crispy onion rings without them becoming greasy.

• For added flavor, you can incorporate spices like cayenne pepper or smoked paprika into the seasoned flour mixture.

• Don't overcrowd the frying pan; fry the onion rings in batches for even cooking and crispiness.

Enjoy your homemade Halal Onion Rings!